9115

Mat. # 800007

purchase Mid America $16.95 2001

THE HOLOCAUST

BEARING WITNESS
AFTER THE HOLOCAUST

Stuart A. Kallen

9115

Published by Abdo & Daughters, 4940 Viking Drive, Suite 622, Edina, Minnesota 55435.

Library bound edition distributed by Rockbottom Books, Pentagon Tower, P.O. Box 36036, Minneapolis, Minnesota 55435.

Printed in the United States.

Cover Photo credit: Bettmann Archives
Interior Photo credits: Bettmann Archives, pages 7, 10, 20, 23, 29,
                32, 35, 38, 41, 43
                Wide World Photos, pages 7, 15, 19, 25
                Archive Photos, pages 17, 25

Edited by Rosemary Wallner

Kallen, Stuart A., 1955-
        Bearing witness : after the Holocaust / Stuart A. Kallen.
            p.   cm. -- (The Holocaust)
        Includes bibliographical references and index.
    ISBN 1-56239-354-5
    1. Holocaust, Jewish (1939-1945)--Juvenile literature. 2. War criminals--Juvenile literature. 3. Holocaust survivors--Juvenile literature. [1. Holocaust, Jewish (1939-1945) 2. War criminals. 3. Holocaust survivors.] I. Title. II. Series: Holocaust (Edina, Minn.)
    D804.3.K33   1994
    940.53' 18--dc20

Table of Contents

Foreword

The Holocaust is a tragic time in world history. It was a time of prejudice and bias turned to hate and the persecution of an ethnic group by persons who came into a position of power, allowing them to carry out that hate.

The Holocaust series depicts what prejudice and biases can lead to; how men, women and children—simply because they were Jewish—died horrible deaths.

When a child is born it has no prejudices. Bias must be learned and someone has to display it.

The goal of this series is to enlighten children and help them recognize the ignorance of prejudice so that future generations will be tolerant, understanding, compassionate, and free of prejudice.

Acknowledgments:

Rabbi Morris Allen
        Beth Jacob Congregation

Dr. Stewart Ross
        Mankato State University

Special Thanks to The United States Holocaust Memorial Museum

CHAPTER ONE

AFTER THE HOLOCAUST

On May 8, 1945, the guns of World War II fell silent. Untold millions lay dead. From London to Moscow, from Greece to the Netherlands, Europe was in ruins. Thirty-three to forty million souls lost their lives in the conflict. Five million Poles died. Twenty million Soviets died. Twenty-one countries were affected. Sixty million European civilians were homeless. Hundreds of towns and villages had been entirely wiped off the map by bombs, rockets, and street fighting.

The architect of the war, Adolf Hitler, lay dead, killed by a self-inflicted bullet to the head. His beloved Nazi party had gone down in flames. Hitler often said that his government would last 1,000 years. It had lasted 12. Under Hitler's watch, Germany, once the jewel of Europe, had been reduced to half junkyard, half graveyard.

Poland lost 15 percent of its population to the war. The Soviet Union lost 10 percent. The United States, Britain, Canada, and France had lost a total of 1,500,000 people, many of them soldiers. But nowhere did the ratio of dead come close to that of the European Jews. Hitler, the Nazis, and their collaborators had killed 2 out of 3 Jewish men, women, and children in Europe—over six million people. And the Jews were not killed as soldiers. They were killed as a civilian population who was exterminated, on purpose, for only one reason—they were Jewish.

Hitler also vented his hatred on Gypsies, homosexuals, and Jehovah's Witnesses. They too were murdered in massive numbers by the Nazis.

When Nazi leader Adolf Hitler became the chancellor of Germany in 1933, he made one thing perfectly clear: Jewish people were, in his words, "vermin, parasites, devils, and disease." Hitler stripped the Jews of their civil rights. He took away their property and businesses. He built concentration camps to imprison and murder Jews and other political foes. He called for the extermination of the Jewish people. Within a few years, 9,000 concentration camps were built to house the prisoners.

By 1940 Hitler and the Germans had overrun Europe. They controlled the Netherlands, Austria, France, Poland, Czechoslovakia, Lithuania, Latvia, Bulgaria, Hungary, and the western Soviet Union.

Every country the Nazis occupied became a killing ground for Jews. In the Netherlands, Jews were packed into railroad trains and sent to concentration camps. In Lithuania and the Soviet Union, mobile death squads stripped Jews naked and shot them in mass graves. Hundreds of thousands died in this manner. In Poland, millions of Jews were herded into tiny walled cities called ghettos. There, they died in the streets of disease and starvation.

By 1942 Hitler was growing impatient with this hit-or-miss destruction of the Jews. It was taking too long. His generals gathered in a Berlin suburb and organized an efficient method for mass murder. The Nazis decided to turn the major concentration camps into death camps. They built poison gas chambers that were disguised as group showers. They built ovens, called crematoria, to burn the dead bodies. Instead of killing the Jews 10,000 at a time, the Nazis could kill millions.

7

British Field Marshall Sir Bernard Montgomery (second from left), commanding the 21st Army Group for the Allied forces.

German civilians of Nordhausen carry dead prisoners from the concentration camp near town for mass burial under supervision of U.S. First Army.

They called their evil plan the "Final Solution to the Jewish Problem."

From 1942 to 1945 the Nazis went on a killing spree unmatched in history. At death camps across Europe millions of people were gassed and their bodies burned. When the Nazis realized they were losing the war in 1944, they redoubled their efforts. They wanted to finish the Final Solution while they still could. Ten thousand people a day were exterminated at Auschwitz. When the ovens could hold no more corpses, they burned the excess in bonfires.

The killing went on until the Nazis could hear the enemy troops within shooting distance. Then they emptied the camps and forced the prisoners on death marches. Those who could not walk were shot where they fell. Those who could walk were marched into the sea and then shot. The Nazis would not give up on the Final Solution until the last minutes of World War II.

CHAPTER TWO

THE LIBERATION

*B*y 1944 Hitler had been losing the war with the Soviet Union for many months. The Soviets reclaimed their country and began to chase the Germans back into Nazi-occupied Poland. Before long, the Soviet Army pushed into Germany and took the Nazi capital of Berlin.

On July 23, 1944, Soviet troops arrived at the death camp of Majdanek, outside the Polish city of Lubin. The SS were busy trying to hide, bury, and burn the evidence of their atrocities. When the Soviets arrived, there were few living prisoners. But plenty of evidence remained, including a mountain of 800,000 pairs of shoes. The soldiers were shocked. A Soviet reporter, Roman Karmann, filed a report:

> In the course of my travels into liberated territory I have never seen a more abominable sight than Majdanek near Lubin... where more than half a million European men, women, and children were massacred....This is not a concentration camp; it is a gigantic murder plant.
>
> Save for the 1,000 living corpses the Red (Soviet) Army found alive when it entered, no inmate escaped alive. Yet full trains daily brought thousands from all parts of Europe to be coldly, brutally massacred.
>
> In the center of the camp stands a huge stone building with a factory chimney—the world's largest crematorium....The

gas chambers contained some 250 people at a time. They were closely packed...so that after they suffocated they remained standing.... It is difficult to believe it myself, but my human eyes cannot deceive me...

Shoes of death camp victims are displayed at the Holocaust Memorial Museum. The shoes are a grim reminder of the brutality that existed at the death camps.

Some of the thousands of wedding rings taken from the victims of the Buchenwald death camp.

In the summer of 1944, the Soviets discovered the camps at Belzac, Treblinka, and Sobibór. These camps had been shut down for a year because the murder of the Polish Jews had been completed. The SS had burned Treblinka and turned it into a farm. Still, soldiers found bones sticking out of the ground.

On January 27, 1945, the Soviets marched into Auschwitz. The last roll call at the camp had been ten days earlier when 67,012 prisoners had been counted. Most of them had been sent on death marches. Before the Soviets arrived, the Nazis frantically tried to take the camp apart. Crematoria were blown up. SS and I. G. Farben (the company that made the gas) burned documents. Still the Soviets discovered 348,820 men's suits, 836,255 women's coats, 13,964 carpets, and seven tons of human hair.

The British liberated Bergen-Belsen camp on April 15, 1945. Thousands of corpses lay rotting in the sun. Sixty thousand prisoners were still alive, many of them in critical condition. Fourteen thousand died during the first days of liberation. Another fourteen thousand died in the weeks that followed. British doctors tried desperately to save them.

The British were horrified with what they found. Mass graves were dug and bulldozers were brought in to shovel the dead. Local civilians were marched through the camp. The British took films that were shown throughout the world. Finally, the workings of Hitler's Final Solution were known to all.

Disease was so rampant in the camp that it had to be burned to the ground. In September 1945, forty-eight members of the Bergen-Belsen staff were tried. Eleven were executed in December.

American troops entered Buchenwald on April 11, 1945. Only days before, twenty-five thousand prisoners were taken out of the camp and sent on a death march. Most died.

Americans liberated other camps in April. A soldier describes the scene at Dachau:

> The American soldiers were furious. Control was gone after the sights we saw, and men were deliberately wounding guards that were available and then turned them over to prisoners and allowed them to take their revenge on them."

SS officers were paraded before the prisoners. The prisoners were asked to judge: good or bad? The judgment was carried out immediately.

The last of the camps liberated by the Americans were Mauthausen and Gusen on May 5, 1945. Three days later, World War II was over in Europe.

The toll on the Jews had been enormous. Six million dead. Ninety percent of the Jews in Poland, Czechoslovakia, Lithuania, and Latvia had been murdered. Over 4,500 cities in 21 countries with Jewish populations were destroyed. The thousand-year-old cultural centers of Jewish thinking had been reduced to smoke and ashes.

CHAPTER THREE

INTO THE LIGHT

*T*he war was over. The survivors of the concentration camps were free. Most were starved and ridden with disease. Those who had been hiding in the woods came out into the light of day. Those who had been living as Christians with false papers returned to being Jews. One Jewish family in Russia had been hiding in a tunnel beneath a pig pen for two years. They came out—white-faced, barely able to walk. In Holland, families who had been hiding in attics for years were able to see the sky again.

All over Europe, dazed Jews awoke from the nightmare. Deprived of newspapers or radios, many didn't know what had happened. They didn't know if their brothers, sisters, mothers, fathers, uncles, aunts, cousins, or lovers were still alive. Most were not. They didn't know what had happened in the next town. Some had never heard the names of Auschwitz, Bergen-Belsen, and other killing centers.

Some Jews had survived. But now what? For the most part, they were still hated in their own countries. Many people blamed them for the war. They had no homes—strangers were living in them. They had no businesses—the Nazis had stolen them and given them to others. They had no families to rely on—whole families had disappeared in the flames. They had no graveyards to visit. The Jewish family of Europe was no more.

At the camps, tens of thousands were still dying. Allied doctors from the United States, Britain, and the Soviet Union could do little more than comfort and watch. The dying would go on for months.

The Allies brought food, clothing, and medical aid to the prisoners who were now called refugees. The death camps were turned into refugee camps. Allied Jewish organizations came to help. The orphaned children were given hope and a bowl of food. Hundreds of thousands of terrorized Jews sat in the camps with nowhere to go.

There had been no help for the millions who perished in the Nazi flames. The handful who escaped had no one to thank except the ending of the war. Slowly they began to leave the camps and build new lives. The Nazis had tattooed many of them with numbers. They would carry those tattooed reminders until the day they died.

Those who had been hiding had someone to thank. The ones who avoided the camps did so with the help of Christians who fed them, hid them, or helped them on their way.

For the survivors, there was a new fear. One survivor of Bergen-Belsen wrote:

> For the great part of the liberated Jews...there was no ecstasy, no joy at our liberation. We had lost our families, our homes. We had no place to go, nobody to hug, nobody who was waiting for us, anywhere. We had been liberated from death and the fear of death, but we were not free from the fear of life.

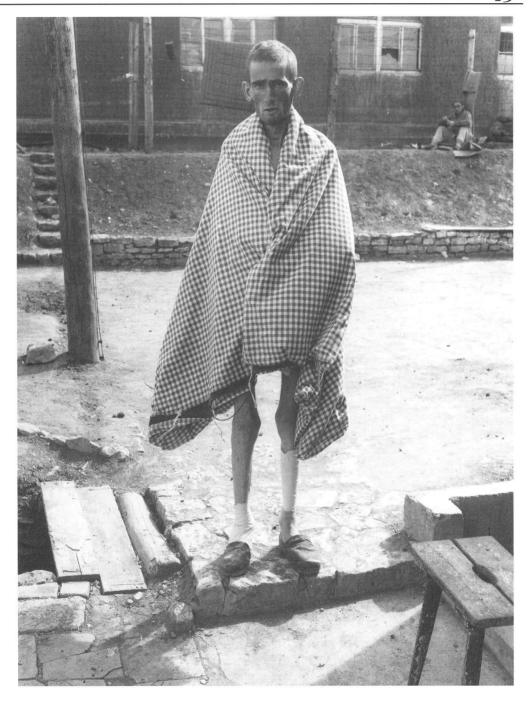

This prisoner of Buchenwald prison camp was freed by the U.S. Third Army. A ghastly illustration of what once represented a man, his condition was so severe it was beyond medical attention.

CHAPTER FOUR

THE TRIALS AT NUREMBERG

*I*n late 1943 Allied leaders Franklin Roosevelt (U.S.), Winston Churchill (Great Britain), and Joseph Stalin (Soviet Union) said that when the war was over they would bring the Nazis to justice. The Allies were outraged at the Nazi treatment of civilians. This anger was fueled when the Allies discovered the killing centers.

The Soviets were the first to discover the camps, at Majdanek. Within weeks they held the first trials of Nazi war criminals.

After the war, an agreement was reached between the Allies to hold joint trials of Nazi leaders. The men would be tried for the killing of civilians. Supreme Court Justice Robert Jackson was named to lead the American prosecution. A team of 600 lawyers, investigators, and aids worked on the cases.

Nuremberg was chosen for the sight of the trials. It was one of the few German cities that was not totally in ruins. It was also the place where Hitler had passed the original laws against the Jews in 1933. Later Nuremberg was host to annual Nazi party pageants where 100,000 German soldiers stood at attention and listened to Hitler's mad ravings while spectators cheered.

The Nazis were to be tried for three kinds of crimes. First, were Crimes Against Peace, which included planning, preparing, starting, and waging a war of aggression.

Top Nazi leaders on trial before an International Tribunal in the Palace of Justice, Nuremburg. (Left to right in the box) Hermann Goering, Rudolf Hess, Joachim von Ribbentrop. (L to R in back row) Admirals Karl Donitz and Brich Raeder.

Then there were War Crimes. This list included murder, ill-treatment of people, deportation of populations for slave labor, killing of hostages and prisoners of war; the plunder of private property, and the destruction of towns and cities.

The third group of crimes were called Crimes Against Humanity. These were defined as murder, extermination, enslavement, or deportation of any civilian population; and persecution on political, racial, or religious grounds, whether or not these acts were legal in the country where they took place. These crimes were prosecuted, it was argued, so that the conscience of the human race could be cleansed.

The first trial began on November 20, 1945. It was an International Military Tribunal. It was seen not only as a trial of Nazis but as a new code of laws for all nations to obey. American military police guarded the huge courtroom, which held 600 people. Translators rendered the gruesome details in four different languages.

Twenty-two major Nazi leaders were indicted. They included Hitler's trusted lieutenant Hermann Goering, Nazi party officials, foreign minister Joachim von Ribbentrop, key cabinet officials, military leaders, the minister of armaments, the minister of labor, and occupation officials. Those later indicted included Hans Frank, the governor-general of Poland, and Fritz Sauckel, who had run the slave-labor program. Some Nazi leaders were not there. Joseph Goebbels had committed suicide after killing his wife and children. Heinrich Himmler killed himself after he was captured.

*Hermann Goering, leader of the Luftwaffe and second in command
of the Reich under Hitler, appears in the "mug shot" of him on file
with the Central Registry of War Criminals in Paris.*

Justice Jackson opened the trial with a statement:

> In the prisoners' dock sit twenty-odd broken men...their
> personal capacity for evil is forever past. It is hard now to
> (see) in these miserable men as captives, the power by
> which—as Nazi leaders—they once dominated much of the
> world and terrified most of it...as individuals their fate is of
> little consequence in the world.

> What makes this inquest significant is that these prisoners...
> are living symbols of racial hatreds, of terrorism and
> violence, and of the arrogance and cruelty of power....
> Civilization can afford no compromise with the social forces
> which would gain renewed strength if we deal...indecisively
> with the men in whom those forces now...survive.

The trial was shocking. Day after day, month after month, a mind-numbing stream of witnesses detailed the German Crimes Against Humanity. Photographs and newsreels showed the nightmare of the Holocaust. The events told of the extermination of Jews, Gypsies, Slavs, and prisoners of war in vile conditions and sickening numbers. They showed the terror and the wide spread use of torture and murder by the Gestapo, the SS, and other official Nazi agencies. Evidence of mass deportation, slave-labor and sadistic medical experiments was presented. The Nazis were also prosecuted for looting national treasures of conquered countries and the private property of imprisoned people. It was almost a limitless list of disgrace.

Considering the circumstances, the trial was conducted in a fair and reasonable manner. In previous times, the men on the stands would have been shot without trial.

The task of collecting the evidence was colossal. Documents on the SS alone filled six freight cars. The final transcripts ran to 10 million words.

Nuremberg trials, December 1945. The judges of the Nuremebrg trials are seen here seated under their respective flags.

The men tried at Nuremberg had little in common. Some were just career politicians. Some were brutal monsters. Goering, who was a drug addict, had lost 120 pounds in prison, deprived of his cream buns and morphine. Still, he had to turn sideways to fit through narrow elevator doors.

The prisoners did not get along well together. They trusted or liked no one. Ribbentrop complained about being tried with Goering. Then he fired his attorney for not wishing him a Happy New Year in 1946. Rudolph Hess marched around the prison yard with a Nazi goose-step. Hess also read novels or slept in court. Goering hissed "Swine!" at a witness he didn't like. Some claimed they couldn't remember anything. One suggested another should be hung for his stupidity. Occasionally, the prisoners laughed at a botched translation.

After a suicide, the prisoners were watched twenty-four hours a day by soldiers. Five American tanks surrounded the prison along with sand-bagged machine gun nests.

The judgment at Nuremberg was in. Three men were sentenced to life in prison. Others were sentenced to 20, 15, or 10 years. The rest were condemned to death by hanging.

In the early hours of October 16, 1946, the doomed men crossed the prison yard to a gymnasium. Eight newspaper writers and 10 witnesses awaited them along with a new gallows. Guards escorted them up the 13 steps to a platform. There they were hung.

Ribbentrop wished "Peace to the world" before he died. Julius Streicher yelled "Heil Hitler!" The American soldier who performed the hanging said later: "I hanged those 10 Nazis and I am proud of it." The bodies of the dead men were cremated.

CHAPTER FIVE

NAZIS AFTER NUREMBERG

*O*ther trials involved Germans who were involved with big business, the security service, the diplomatic corps, the officer corps, and so on. Every trial produced new evidence that led to more arrests and more trials. Men and women who had taken up normal lives as businesspeople, lawyers, doctors, clerks, and laborers were arrested. In the American courts alone, 199 people were tried between July 1945 and July 1949. Of those, 18 were executed and 23 were sentenced to life in prison. In American courts at Dachau, near the death camp, 420 Germans were sentenced to death. Over the next 20 years, Allied and German courts convicted over 20,000 Nazis.

Meanwhile over 100,000 Germans were summoned before Allied "de-Nazification" courts. The court's object was to erase every trace of Nazism from Germany. Those courts handed out fines or prison sentences. Some were barred from ever working in government.

The task of "de-Nazifiying" Germany was huge. The Americans issued 12 million forms containing 131 questions. The questions asked about a person's past life and associations. These were given to every person over 18 years of age in the American zone. (Germany had been divided into four zones, one each to the Americans, French, British, and Soviet Union.) As a result of the survey, 169,282 people were tried for the past Nazi and military activities.

Most of those caught later were small-time Nazis. Over 20,000 of the most-wanted Nazis had escaped to Egypt, Syria, the Middle East, or South America. The countries of Argentina and Paraguay granted these criminals political asylum. Many had engineered their escapes before the German collapse. They stole huge sums of money, false papers, and useful addresses abroad. Some escaped using the same agencies set up to help the Jews and other war refugees.

One Nazi escape route was so commonly used that it earned the nickname "the Rat Line." The route went from Austria and Bavaria, over the mountains into Italy, and from there by ship to South America. The escaping "rats" were helped by a group called ODESSA, an organization of SS men set up for this purpose.

Nuremberg citizens crowd around to read the results of the war trials in the local papers October 1, 1946.

CHAPTER SIX

THE BIG FISH ESCAPE THE NET

*A*mong those who escaped were the two most wanted Nazis of all—Franz Stangl, commandant of the Sobibor and Treblinka death camps; and Adolf Eichmann, who was responsible for running the entire Nazi Jewish extermination program.

Stangl was responsible for killing over one million people. The Americans captured him shortly after the war ended and put him in a prison camp in Austria. Stangl managed to escape in 1948 and made his way to Italy. There he obtained a passport from a German bishop. Soon, Stangl made his way to Syria. In 1951 he moved to Brazil with his family.

Once in Brazil, Stangl—murderer of millions—found work as an engineer in a Volkswagen automobile factory. Using his real name, Stangl lived a comfortable life in São Paulo, Brazil, until he was arrested in 1967. More than 20 years after running one of the most horrifying death camps in history, Stangl was shipped back to Germany to stand trial for his crimes. He died in a Düsseldorf prison in 1971.

Adolph Eichmann was one of the most dreaded criminals of the Nazi era. He was the head of the Nazi Central Security Service. Eichmann was the chief of operations and oversaw the entire program of mass extermination against the Jews.

At the end of the war, Eichmann was hiding in Austria. American troops arrested him but they did not know who he was. The Americans put Eichmann in a prison camp for Nazis. There, he was well known by the other inmates. Eichmann's fellow prisoners helped him escape in 1946.

Undated photo of Adolf Eichmann, the Nazi in charge of the Jewish bureau. Notice the skull and crossbones on his hat, the symbol of the SS.

Former SS Colonel Adolf Eichmann had been apprehended by Israeli police. In 1960 Eichmann was put on trial in Israel for war crimes. He is considered to be responsible for the death of six million Jews.

9115

Eichmann's name began to crop up often at the Nuremberg trials. For the next four years, Eichmann worked as a lumberjack near Hamburg, Germany. He used the name Otto Heninger. In early 1950 Eichmann followed the Rat Line and fled to Argentina. Once there, the mastermind of the death camps worked in a laundry and on a rabbit farm. His wife and children joined him in 1952.

Eichmann started his first steady job as a mechanic at a Mercedes-Benz factory. He lived a dreary life in a poor section of Buenos Aires. The Germans who lived in the area knew who he was, but Eichmann did not try to hide. In 1960 Israeli secret agents caught up with Eichmann and took him to Israel to stand trial. Eichmann died by hanging in 1962.

By 1950 other world events had driven the Nazi trials out of the public mind. Many Germans were clamoring for release of those Nazis already convicted. The Pope asked for mercy for Nazi officials condemned to die. In 1951 the American high command in Germany granted clemency to all but five Nazis who participated in the mass killings. Seventy-seven Nazi officials were freed. Some of the owners of factories that had used slave labor had their businesses and their fortunes returned to them.

In the end the trials only touched a small number of top Nazi leaders. Most who were responsible for the Holocaust escaped punishment.

CHAPTER SEVEN

THE RATS COME TO AMERICA

*A*fter the war, over 10,000 Nazi war criminals moved to the United States. They were brought in by the government who, by then, was afraid of the Soviet Union taking over Europe. In the words of Alan Ryan, former director of a U.S. government spy agency, "They came in through the front door with their papers in order."

The Joint Chiefs of Staff are the people who oversee all branches of the U.S. military. In the 1950s the Joint Chiefs ran a program called "Operation Paperclip." That program brought 1,600 German and Austrian scientists and technicians—including war criminals—to the United States. The former Nazis were put to work for NASA, the National Security Agency (NSA), the Central Intelligence Agency (CIA), the military, and other organizations.

Arthur Rudolph, who directed the Saturn V moon rocket project, used slave labor at the Dora concentration camp. At Dora, Rudolph was trying to build high-powered V-2 rockets to help the Nazis take over the world. The famous rocket scientist Werner Von Braun also used Jewish slave labor in concentration camps before coming to the United States to work for NASA.

Operation Paperclip was imitated by universities and private industry. A Romanian religion professor at the University of Chicago had written propaganda papers during the war urging Romanians to kill all Jews. A Russian language teacher at Yale had performed the same task for the Nazis.

I. G. Farben is a huge petrochemical company in Germany. It could be compared in size with Standard Oil in America. During the war, I. G. Farben ran its own concentration camp at Auschwitz, using slave labor to manufacture its products. Most importantly, I. G. Farben made the prussic acid gas, Zyklon B, that was used to gas six million Jews and five million other people in the death camps. One of the men who ran I. G. Farben was Otto Ambros. After the war, Ambros became a member of the board at the American corporation W. R. Grace.

CHAPTER EIGHT

THE DP CAMPS

*A*fter World War II, over 10 million people were living in countries that were not their own. They were called "Displaced Persons," or DPs. Jewish survivors had nowhere to go. Many were forced to live in the concentration camps that had been their nightmare for so long. For many this meant staying in Germany among the people who had tried to kill them.

The U. S. Army had its hands full trying to oversee its occupation of Germany. This was coupled with the demands for housing, medicine, and food from the Jewish survivors. The army had no long-range plans to deal with the problems of those who could not or would not go home.

Life in the DP camps was hard. The people who had to live there were depressed. They were haunted by nightmares and trusted no one—not even the Americans who were trying to help them. Other people who lived in the camps openly hated the Jews in their midst. There was food, but it was bad, and there was very little of it.

One man who ran a DP camp wrote:

> The camp is filthy beyond description. Sanitation is virtually unknown....The army units we relieved did nothing more than insure rations (food) were delivered to the camp....The people of the camp appear demoralized and beyond hope of rehabilitation. They appear to be beaten, both spiritually and physically.

At Belsen death camp, 1945, a living skeleton is seen delousing his clothes.

CHAPTER NINE

SPECIAL STATUS

*M*ost Jewish DPs wanted to begin new lives in Palestine. That was, after all, the place where the Jewish religion had begun over 4,000 years before. It was also the place that the Jews had been driven out of in A.D. 70. Since that time, the Jews had wandered the earth, facing anti-Semitism almost everywhere. That is how they ended up in Europe to face the Final Solution almost 2,000 years later.

But Great Britain ruled the country of Palestine and refused to let the Jews move there. The Arab nations in the area hated the Jews and Britain needed their oil.

In 1945, U.S. President Harry Truman sent Earl Harrison to report on the displaced-persons camps. Harrison was the Dean of the University of Pennsylvania Law School. His report to Truman was a bombshell. He wrote:

> We (the United States) appear to be treating the Jews as the Nazis treated them, except that we do not exterminate them. They are in concentration camps in large numbers under our military guard instead of SS troops. One (wonders) whether the German people seeing this are not supposing that we are following...Nazi policy.

Harrison recommended that the Jews be given special status because of the Holocaust. He said they should be evacuated from Germany immediately. Harrison also said that 100,000 Jews should be allowed to move to Palestine.

Truman supported Harrison's report. He began to pressure Britain to allow Jews into Palestine. He also opened the U.S. borders to a limited number of Jewish immigrants. Truman said: "It is unthinkable that the Jews be left [permanently] in camps in Europe."

The British responded by saying:"The Americans want 100,000 Jews in Palestine because they don't want them in New York."

Meanwhile, Jewish relief agencies began pouring into the DP camps. They started schools and taught Hebrew, agriculture, and other skills. Children were born and Jewish religious services resumed. Over 70 newspapers in dozens of languages began publication. Survivors of families found each other. Hundreds of schools were formed to begin teaching 12,000 students. Collective farms were formed. All of the hubbub of life in the camps had one main purpose—to prepare people for life in Palestine.

On July 10, 1946, a mob of Poles attacked 150 Jews who had returned to the town of Kielce (pronounced Key-el-se). Forty-two were killed and 50 wounded. The Jews were survivors who had returned to Kielce to look for their families. Over 24,000 Jews had lived in the town before the Holocaust. Appeals were made to church leaders to stop the violence. The church remained silent. The only priest in town who protested was removed from his pulpit within a week. When the police were called, they took away the few weapons that the Jews had.

News of the Kielce attack spread through the Jewish community like wildfire. It was as though nothing had changed. Jews in Poland knew there was no safe return to home. Within months, 100,000 Jews fled Poland. They flooded into the DP camps. The Soviet Union also allowed its Jews to migrate, releasing over 100,000.

All over Eastern Europe, Jews flooded into American-occupied Germany. Something had to be done.

In 1948 the U.S. Congress passed an immigration law that would allow 200,000 DPs into America over four years. But the law discriminated against Jews. Half the immigrants it let in were Roman Catholic. Only 16 percent were Jewish. In 1950, the law was changed slightly to allow more Jews into America. By then it was too late. Most had gone to Israel.

Israeli Prime Minister David Ben-Gurion reads a proclamation declaring existence of a new Jewish state in Jerusalem, May 1948.

CHAPTER TEN

EXODUS TO PALESTINE

*B*etween 1944 and 1948 over 200,000 Jews fled Eastern and Central Europe to Palestine. They crossed borders legally, illegally, or "semi-legally." Most countries were glad to get rid of the Jews and instructed the border guards to look the other way.

The movement began small, one person at a time. But one by one, the tiny trickle turned into a flood of Jews into Palestine. The movement was given a name—Bricha—the Hebrew word for escape.

Meanwhile, the Jews were not about to wait for political solutions to their problems. Aided by underground networks and Jews working in Europe and in the American military, boatload after boatload escaped to Palestine. The British Royal Navy stopped many of the ships. They sent the passengers to detention camps in Cyprus.

The Mossad, an organization that later became the Israeli Secret Service, operated many of the ships. The Mossad notified journalists of leaving ships; the journalists came along for the ride. When the British captured boatloads of Holocaust survivors and imprisoned them, yet again, the photographers snapped pictures. When the world saw the pictures, the British were forced to reexamine their policies.

The most famous event was the journey of the ship *Exodus,* 1947. The passengers on the ship came from Poland, Germany, Hungary, and other nations. Many were "Jews of the miracle"—inmates in death camps who had somehow survived.

On July 18, 1947, the boat arrived in Haifa, Palestine. The passengers were singing as they descended the gangplank to touch the soil of freedom. The arrival should have been a dream fulfilled. Instead it turned into a nightmare.

The 4,554 men, women, and children aboard the *Exodus* were illegal immigrants in Palestine. The British decided to make an example of them. The British Royal Navy had dogged the ship on its long journey. As the ship neared Haifa, two British destroyers rammed it and 40 marines and sailors rushed aboard. A battle raged for three hours. Desperate passengers pitched tins of canned meat at soldiers who hit them with billy clubs and sprayed them with tear gas. When the British won, two refugees were dead. A crew member died later.

The ship's captain was arrested and the passengers were taken to British transport ships. In a move that shocked the world, the British decided to take the concentration camp survivors back to Germany.

In Haifa the Jews were separated from their baggage and then from one another—much like the Nazis had done. Then soldiers strip searched the men. Arab women searched the Jewish women. The soldiers sprayed all of them with the pesticide DDT to delouse them. They took cameras and smashed them. Water bottles were also smashed on the dock.

The prisoners did not give up yet. Many had to be carried kicking and screaming to waiting prison ships. Forty-one people managed to slip away to freedom. When the remaining prisoners reached France, they refused to get off the ships. The British waited for hunger and heat to drive the Jews off the ship. But for five weeks, the Jews refused to leave the prison ship.

Israeli's Prime Minister, David Ben-Gurion, with his wife and friends at the Haifa docks to see the last contigent of British troops leave the Holy Land. This marks the beginning of a new Jewish homeland, 1948.

One observer wrote of the conditions:

> Imagine yourself on the New York subway. It's August, it's rush hour. They've turned off the fans, slammed the doors, and you're left standing up against each other for five weeks.

At dawn on September 8, 1947—almost two months after leaving Haifa—the prison ship arrived in Hamburg, Germany. The British assembled 2,500 soldiers with batons and tear gas. Six medical squads stood by. By then, many defeated passengers got off the ship. But 1,485 refused. Eventually, they were dragged off, kicking, screaming, and spitting at the soldiers.

Once off the ships, prison trains took the Holocaust survivors to two camps outside of Hamburg. One camp had been built by the Nazis to house slave laborers. The other was built by the British. Both had armed guards, searchlights, and barbed wire. Inside, people were jammed into tents and huts. Many refused to eat. The British interrogated the Jews but they refused to answer. When asked where they were from, they screamed "Palestine!"

After a few months, the British jailers got bored and lax. One by one, the Jewish prisoners slipped away. Most doggedly returned to Palestine. Within a year, all of them were gone.

CHAPTER ELEVEN

THE LAND OF ISRAEL

*O*n May 18, 1948, the nation of Israel was born. The British flag was taken down and in its place rose the blue and white Star of David flag. That evening, Israel was attacked by five Arab countries. A Jewish army was in place to fend off the attack.

In the Israeli Declaration of Independence, the new state ended all restrictions on Jewish immigration. The Israeli government evacuated camps in Cyprus and the DP camps all over Europe. It also began recruiting young, able-bodied people for the Israeli Defense Forces. Some of the soldiers had fought the Nazis in underground armies during the war.

By fall of 1949, Jews were leaving the DP camps in Europe at a rate of 10,000 a month. All who wanted to move to Israel did so. Other Jews arrived from Iraq, Syria, Lebanon, Egypt, and North Africa where they had been persecuted. In 1950 Israel granted Jews immediate citizenship upon their arrival. The people who were unwanted everywhere now had a place to call home.

The task of building a country was difficult. There were cities to build and crops to plant. And there were wars to be fought with the Arabs. All this activity helped the survivors to put the past behind them. Still, the haunting memories of death camps could not be easily erased.

The state of Israel became the most positive thing to come from the Holocaust. The arrival of the displaced persons and the concentration camp survivors increased support and sympathy for the Jewish state worldwide. But Israel could never undo the horrors of the Holocaust.

In Jerusalem, Feburary 1949, Dr. Chaim Weizmann is inaugurated as the first President of the new state of Israel. At right, front row, is David Ben-Gurion, head of the Labor party.

CHAPTER TWELVE

IS HITLER DEAD?

*T*he ideas that moved Adolf Hitler and the Nazis to murder all the Jews did not die with him. Those who follow in his footsteps do not have his power. But they continue to desecrate Jewish cemeteries and monuments. And they still launch attacks on residents of Jewish neighborhoods. In the past 20 years, extreme right-wing parties have emerged with ideas taken directly from Nazi writings. This trend includes the French National Front and its British counterpart. There are also many European newspapers in the hands of anti-Semitic right-wingers.

Since the mid-1970s a growing number of people have been writing scholarly books that deny the Holocaust ever happened. These works have surfaced in the United States, France, Germany, and Great Britain.

In 1979 an organization calling itself the "Institute of Historical Review," based in San Diego, California, offered a prize of $50,000 to anyone who could prove that the Holocaust really happened. A survivor named Mel Mermelstein took up the challenge. His claim was verified by American courts. The institute, not surprisingly, refused to hand over the money. After a court battle, the institute was forced to pay Mermelstein.

But the institute has a branch in Britain that goes door to door and to schools handing out anti-Semitic literature.

After World War II, Germany was divided in half. The western half was a democratic nation. The eastern half was run by a Communist dictatorship. In 1989, the Berlin Wall fell, and

Germany was once again reunited. The East Germans who had been living in a time warp since the war were suddenly able to speak their minds. What some of them had to say frightened the world.

Many of the newly freed Germans were poor and unemployed. Once again they started blaming their problems on the Jews. Old Nazi propaganda films showing Jewish people as rats overrunning the world were widely distributed. More than 80,000 young men and women shaved their heads and became Nazi skinheads.

In addition to the skinheads, the extreme right-wing German Republican party began to flex its muscle, picking up representation in the German parliament. Their platform is frighteningly like the Nazis. The neo-Nazis consider themselves patriotic Germans and have joined the German Republicans. They have attacked and killed foreign workers, burned houses and brought back the shrill anti-Semitism of the past.

Kurt Waldheim was an intelligence officer for the Austrian Nazis. He later became the Secretary-General of the United Nations by denying his past. When Waldheim ran for president of Austria in 1985, Jewish people revealed that he was once a Nazi. A wave of anti-Semitism swept through Austria, once again targeting Jews. Newspapers and television blamed the Jews for problems in Austria. By then, there were only 8,000 Jews left from the 200,000 who lived there before the war. Nonetheless, Nazism reared its ugly head in Austria once again.

Anti-Semitism and Nazism is also on the rise in Poland, the Soviet Union, and other newly freed Communist nations. With the fall of Communism, tens of thousands of Soviet Jews emigrated to Israel.

*David Ben-Gurion and other Jewish leaders as they addressed
a gathering of Jews from the balcony of the Jewish Agency
Building, after the UN partition plan for Palestine had been
announced, December 1947.*

CHAPTER THIRTEEN

REMEMBRANCE

*A*s time passes, eye witnesses to the Holocaust have begun to die of old age. As the ones who remember die, phony scholars try to deny what happened. The neo-Nazis have no memory of the horrors of World War II. With their ignorance of history, they begin to repeat it.

As for the Jewish people, they will never forget. The United States Holocaust Memorial Museum in Washington, D.C., and movies like *Schindler's List* will help the world remember.

If there is any lesson in the Holocaust it is how fragile democracy can be. It proves how important it is for all of us to defend the ideals of dignity, freedom, and justice, even when it affects people other than ourselves. For in the end, no people can be free if some people are denied their freedom.

The interior of the Tel Aviv museum in December of 1948 when the new state of Israel proclaimed its independence in a proclamation read by David Ben-Gurion, Prime Minister.

GLOSSARY

Allies - the United States, the Soviet Union, Great Britain, France, Canada and the other countries who came together to fight Germany, Italy, and Japan in World War II.

Anti-Semitism - hatred of Jews.

Asylum - protection given to political offenders who have fled their home countries.

Atrocity - a shockingly bad or atrocious act.

Auschwitz - the largest and most highly organized Nazi death camp. Auschwitz was nineteen square miles and guarded by 6,000 men. Over 1,250,000 people were murdered at Auschwitz, 90 percent of them Jewish.

Clemency - mercy or forgiveness for crimes committed.

Collaborator - a person who works with an enemy nation. People who helped the Nazis after the Nazis invaded their country were collaborators. Some were spies who gave important information to the Nazis.

Concentration camps - a guarded camp for the detention and forced labor of political prisoners.

Cremate, crematoria - to cremate is to burn a dead body; this is done in a crematorium; more than one crematorium are crematoria.

Demoralize - to deprive of the spirit and courage to continue living.

Deportation - to expel from a city, region, or country

Desecrate - to ruin, spoil, or foul a sacred object.

Evacuate - to remove for reasons of safety.

Exodus - a mass moving of people, from the Bible story Exodus that tells of Jews following Moses out of Egypt.

Exterminate - to destroy totally.

Gestapo - the German state secret police.

Ghetto - a section of a city in most European countries where all Jews were forced to live.

Holocaust - the mass extermination of Jews by Nazis.

Liberate - to free.

Persecute - to harass someone with harsh treatment because of their race, religion, or beliefs.

Propaganda - information or ideas that are repeated over and over to change the public's thinking about an idea or group of people.

Refugee - a person who flees to a foreign country during a war hoping to find peace or refuge.

Right-wing - political faction that is super-patriotic and often intolerant of foreigners. Hitler and the Nazis were known as extreme right-wingers.

Schutzstaffel (SS) - the black-shirted security squad of elite Nazis.

Semite - a member of any of a various ancient and modern people, especially Hebrews or Arabs.

BIBLIOGRAPHY

Adler, David A. *We Remember the Holocaust.* New York: Henry Holt and Company, 1989.

Aharoni, Yohanan, and Avi-Yonah, Michael. *The Macmillan Bible Atlas*. New York: Macmillan, 1993.

Ausubel, Nathan, and Gross, David C. *Pictorial History of the Jewish People.* New York: Crown Publishers, Inc., 1953, 1984.

Berenbaum, Michael. *The World Must Know.* Boston: Little, Brown and Company, 1993.

Block, Gay, and Drucker. *Malka Rescuers.* New York: Holmes & Meier Publications, Inc., 1992

Chaikin, Miriam. A *Nightmare in History: The Holocaust 1933-1945.* New York: Clarion Books, 1987.

Dawidowicz, Lucy S. *The War Against the Jews 1933-1945.* New York: Seth Press, 1986.

Flannery, Edward H. *The Anguish of the Jews.* New York: Paulist Press, 1985.

Gilbert, Martin. *Final Journey*. New York: Mayflower Books, 1979.

Gilbert, Martin. *The Macmillan Atlas of the Holocaust.* New York: Macmillan, 1982.

Greenfeld, Howard. *The Hidden Children.* New York: Ticknor & Fields, 1993.

Landau, Elaine. *The Warsaw Ghetto Uprising.* New York: New Discovery Books, 1992.

Paldiel, Mordecai. *The Path of the Righteous.* Hoboken, New Jersey: KTAV Publishing House, Inc., 1993.

Index